the
human
genome
{poetry}
project

by shruthi n. shivkumar

DEDICATION

dedicated to all that we can never seem to put into words.

CONTENTS

ACKNOWLEDGMENTS

thank you to my parents, for always supporting me despite my
unending series of half-finished creative endeavors and partially-
conceived ideas;
my friends, for dealing with the shreds of writing i incessantly
share, at the most inopportune times;
and my teachers, for constantly encouraging me to explore the
world and follow the words.

introduction:
the human genome poetry project

you have probably heard of the
original Human Genome Project-
the scientific undertaking to sequence every
part and parcel of a human's genome:
but this is a project of a different kind.
it consists of a series of poems that
are inspired by genetics: a seemingly
specific field that forms the foundation
required to create life as we know it.

humans have a range of 24 different chromosomes:
22 different "autosomes", and 2 sex chromosomes,
with women having an X and X,
and men having an X and a Y.

humans have two copies of chromosomes 1-22,
resulting in a grand total of 46 chromosomes.

for every chromosome from 1-22, i picked
a gene found on each one and wrote a piece
inspired by it. after the first 22 poems, you'll find
musings on both the X and Y chromosomes,
as well as an "epilogue" on epigenetics-
the study of what lies *above* the genome.

this collection is meant to demonstrate
that science and art are not isolated, but rather,
different ways of examining *us*.
i hope this chapbook inspires you to
further explore the stuff that
we are made of, and pushes you
to make your own unique connections, as
farfetched and metaphorical as they seem.

happy reading.

background

DNA: short for "deoxyribonucleic acid", carrier of genetic material found in the nucleus of cells

chromosome: threadlike structures of nucleic acids and proteins that carry genetic material- the "packaging" of DNA

gene: an inherited informational unit transferred from parent to offspring that codes for some specific protein, leading to the expression of various traits- found on chromosomes

the human genome poetry project

the twenty-two

autosomes

chromosome 1: 2000-2100 genes
notable gene: ASPM, determinant of brain size

what defines intelligence?

is it genetic? a direct function of human inheritance?
nucleotides that translate to a larger and denser brain,
physically packed with the congested traffic
of "smarter" neuronal highways?

maybe the number of brain cells does not even matter.

what if it is as howard gardener once spoke:
that there are nine types of intelligence -
kinesthetic, linguistic, interpersonal, et cetera -
and everyone hones their own type,
independent of neural density and
the speed limits of their mental networks?

i know what intelligence is not.

it is not grades and tests perpetrated by
school systems that prefer to reduce the
qualitative to the quantitative. it does not
correspond to international test rankings,
and halfhearted metrics of the CollegeBoard.

intelligence is the flexibility of the mind, the
creativity in observing the world, picking it apart,
and stitching together an entirely new idea,
through emotions or math or words or movement.

intelligence, while perhaps partially inherited,
is not reducible to a gene on a chromosome.
intelligence, despite common misconceptions,
is not a number.

chromosome 2: 1300-1400 genes
notable gene: LCT, digestion of lactose products

it's interesting that many believe
lactose intolerance to be abnormal. in fact,
lactose *tolerance* past infancy is a mutation;
LCT is meant to be turned off shortly after
that human phase of dependence, during which
we are sustained by the milk of our mothers.

by some action of nature, genetic mutations led
a lucky few to enjoy familiar dairy products
well into adulthood, and our food-loving
environment encouraged the adaptation.

but some can't help it- throughout the lifetime,
many people begin to rattle the chains of our
original genetics, and those dairy treats begin
transforming into sources of nausea and pain
as LCT switches off, as it was once supposed to.

optimistically i'd say that memories of
melted ice cream on sticky fingertips in summer
curdle at the sight of dairy in later years because
it's a sign of independence and aged wisdom, the ability
to move past the tangible pleasures of crème brûlée
and chocolate milk as we grow older.

pessimistically i'd say that those treats which once
gave us joy, these socially accustomed luxuries which
hurt the body that is supposed to protect us,
are signs of adulthood shocking us with its sudden reality.
that which once seemed satisfying is now
forcing our own fallible anatomy against us.

realistically i'd say it's mother nature's way of telling us to
move on.

chromosome 3: 1000-1100 genes
notable gene: COL7A1, skin collagen

this gene codes for some of the many proteins that
wrap themselves into triple-stranded, braid-like ropes;
which are processed into strong bundles to serve as pillars that
support the intricate yet powerful architecture of our skin.

these dancing, interwoven fibrils of collagen tie the
epidermis to the dermis, knitting together the layers
of our body's largest organ.

your skin is a perfectly complex example of every part
aligning just right; proof of Mother Nature
conducting a symphonic orchestra of molecules, that
come together in a network to form a protective shield
and guard you from the hazards of the exterior.

your DNA has carefully directed the construction of
this lattice-like protector, a construction greater than
the mere sum of its parts. after all that biology has
seen through, after all the chance events that have led to
you and your biological bodyguard,

you deserve to feel comfortable in your skin.
let no one get under it.

chromosome 4: 1000-1100 genes
notable gene: PHOX2B gene, Ondine's Curse

sleep is relaxing for most of us, for you.
and at night you lie in bed, your breaths
moving rhythmically as your chest
falls and rises with the tides,
wait. one breath falls slightly short,
but the automatic parts of your body
quickly right the ship, signaling you
to wake up or breathe more.

the story is different for those with
a mutated PHOX2B gene. sleep is not
synonymous with dreams and relaxation.
instead their shallow, shallow breaths fly
undetected by autonomous radars,
and the ship begins to tilt drastically.

hypoxia. carbon dioxide builds up
precariously and oxygen struggles to
hold on. all because of ondine's curse.

ondine, the water nymph, sacrificed
her immortality in exchange for the love
of handsome palemon. but when she found
him lying with another, kissing another with
the very breath that he once used to pledge
eternal faith to ondine, she spat angrily:

"so you shall breathe when awake. but if you are
are ever to succumb to sleep, your breaths will arrest."

he never slept again. ondine wanted him to suffocate in guilt.
but today, the innocent sufferers of this mutation known as
"Ondine's Curse" require machines to stay alive, while carrying out
the act that everyone else finds peaceful.

chromosome 5: 900 genes
notable gene: IL13, allergic rhinitis {*hay fever*}

one member of the multi-gene squadron that
spurs my Claritin-seeking habits each March 21st.

seasonal allergies are so tedious.

my mother always tells this one story:
i went to my best friend's house to play,
frolicking lightly in her backyard swing set,
and when i returned home, my little
five-year-old face was all swollen like a pufferfish,
and high-pitched sneezes racketed my tiny body.

apparently, i looked like something
out of a cartoon...

later, we found out that i was allergic to
six types of grass, a handful of trees,
and nearly everything outdoors and green.

oh DNA, i don't understand why you made my
systems so paranoid. why does a little pollen
warrant a full fledged immune response featuring
sniffles and tears and coughs and the works?

just let me smell this sweet rose. i'll just get a
little closer. i promise there's nothing to fear-
i can almost smell it; just a few inches,
don't fail me now, faulty antibodies -

ACH-*hoo!*

ugh.

every single time...

chromosome 6: 1000-1100 genes
notable gene: HLA-DQA1, Celiac Disease

the miracle of gluten-laden bread.
it is easy for those of us without
the Celiac disease mutation to
underappreciate the presence of
this multifaceted food in our world...

in the 17th century, the French were
so fond of this magic little carbohydrate
that they baked and seasoned stale pieces into
flavorful croutons that, to this day, top our salads.

need more proof? the baseline
literally used as the *greatest thing since*
was formed in the early 20th century by
an ingenious Otto Rohweder, altering the
course of loaves and sandwiches forever.

and now, allergen-free breads roam the
shelves of specialty stores, so
even those with a Celiac mutation
may enjoy that sweet grain that
we hold near and dear.

but perhaps the most miraculous fact is that
carbon, the organic foundation of bread
(and nearly everything else edible)
cycles through our atmosphere: so, the atoms
making up the sandwich you eat might have once
been breathed out of the lungs of a dinosaur,
affixed in the throes of an ancient sunflower,
or housed in the first crouton.

chew on *that* food for thought.

chromosome 7: 900-1000 genes
notable gene: FOXP2, language and speech production

one of the keys to humanity lies in the units of
meaning that we form in our minds and release
into the world with a final burst of air.

all animals house this special gene, and the human
version differs at only 2 of its 740 units from
that of chimpanzees- our mute relatives.

so this tiny change gives us the unique ability to
produce words, tell stories, share thoughts
otherwise lost in the crevices of a
past generation's mind.

this timeless tool, upon which entire
civilizations were built, allows speakers
to eloquently mesh words to their liking,
permits actors to catapult dialogues from the
stage, and gives us the gift of language.

FOXP2, tell me *your* story, of how your evolving
existence has molded ours, of your permanence
in every facet of life, from the smallest exchange
to the most important political address.

must we thank you for donning the
boon of communication on our fallible,
fragile shoulders? or break under the
pressure of this nearly impossible responsibility?
why, of all the choices, would you handpick
homo sapiens as your recipient?

little things may be easily forgotten.
but
i shall speak wisely henceforth.

chromosome 8: 700 genes
notable gene: PolB, DNA polymerase beta

this gene codes for the protein carrying out
"base excision repair"- whiteout, for nucleic errors.

like keyboard word-replacement,
this enzyme hastens the removal of
imperfections, and rights mutations
of the violet sunlight before we
ever have a chance to feel the mistake.

have you ever imagined how wonderful
it would be to have an autocorrect
for our day-to-day slip-ups?

your coffee would have had
a tightly capped lid on it before you
spilled it all over your shirt that morning.
you never would have sent that half-baked joke
that made no waves in the silent group chat.
you most certainly never would have
done that cringey awful klutz thing that
still haunts you every time you see a
water fountain or a barista named Alex
or a pretzel kiosk or a certain address,

but I guess without those mistakes
we would have no funny stories,
no more meet-cutes or friendships
forged out of mutual awkwardness,
no blushing smiles to look back on,

and I guess with a real-life autocorrect
or macrocosmic DNA Polymerase Beta
we wouldn't really be wonderfully,
awkwardly human.

chromosome 9: 800-900 genes
notable gene: ABO, determinant of blood type

they say that blood is thicker than water,
almost as if the family inheritance passed
down through alphabetic tags of
A's, B's, and O's, is a sign of
fathers and mothers and grandparents.

so, really, every ounce of crimson
circulating through my heart head and toes
is a fragment of family, a gift
from a previous generation recycled
through my system with every
breath and step i take.

and with every blood cell i learn
of my relatives' ABO's.

A: all of the extended family
living on the other half of the world
that i never got to meet.

B: becoming someone i'm not,
only to take a deep breath, remembering
those roots, pausing to tug on
twig-like heart strings and
tireless veins.

O: occasionally calling family, hearing their
voices for the first or thousandth time,
my circulatory system renewed with
love and energy each conversation.

i might not know their names or their favorite colors
or any intimate details of their lives, but i feel them with every
heartbeat.

chromosome 10: 700-800 genes
notable gene: CCAR1, cell cycle & apoptosis regulator

apoptosis: cell death.
preprogrammed suicide of
a little unit of life - harmful,
currently redundant, unneeded,
and insignificant in the
grand scheme of an organism.

at first glance, apoptosis
seems to be a tragedy.

cells, gone, with no mourning.
it appears to be a most blunt
termination, but

after secondary
consideration, and a
fresh glance, it becomes
apparent that apoptosis is
something else completely.

cell suicide is nature's way
of pruning once-helpful pieces
that now prove harmful,
of getting rid of the negative;
the DNA's way of blocking
toxicity- ignoring piercing
words of doubt from the
entities restraining you.

if molecular biology can do that for us so reliably,
why can't we do it with ourselves?

chromosome 11: 1300-1400 genes
notable gene: USH1C, harmonin protein (cochlear hair cells)

a building block of the
tiny invisible organs that
manage our systems,
auditory and vestibular.

these small filaments
translate the pulses of
sound vibration into
a neural signal that allows
us to hear anything from
a hit song to a friend's words,
a piano composition to the
blurry noise of city streets.
your inner ear's structures
translate the world into
a chaotic but constant message.

and they right your mind after
you spin in circles as a child,
rapidly approaching dizziness,
or when you lose your footing
later on in life, your
surroundings quickly blending
into stripes of green and blue.
your inner ear provides you
with balance, harmony,
steadfastness in rotating earth.

big things.

all carried out by the
hair cells' petite *stereocilia*,
only measuring up to a few
millionths of a meter in length:

little things.

chromosome 12: 1100-1200 genes
notable gene: AVPR1a, altruistic or ruthless behavior

the length of this tiny piece of DNA
can affect social behavior drastically. the
longer your AVPR1a sequence, the more likely
you are to donate to pastel-laden charities
or feel sympathy for the neglected
animals on your television.
the shorter your sequence,
the more likely you are to behave selfishly.

can you imagine a world running on the
fuel of this altruism gene? where all people
thought of each other as much of themselves,
where cooperation and empathy
formed a social network of humans ready
to work towards a common goal?

it's not fiction at all. anthropology, the story of us,
repeatedly relays one familiar tale: part of what has
always made us special is our ability to
think selflessly, for the good of the community.

today as we drown in endless fragments of
red and blue, in warring online
battles of opinions, in fiery strawman
debates of the media, remind yourself of
this special human gene, and its purpose.

regardless of your AVPR1a's length, live
everyday as if you have been bestowed with
a long altruistic sequence, a generous heart- even
if your real biology may say otherwise.

remember what allowed humans to make it this far. and imagine
where we are to go.

chromosome 13: 300-400 genes
notable gene: GJB6, gap junction beta protein (connexin)

cell comes from the word
cellula meaning "small rooms"...
in essence, we are all made up of
billions of apartments and houses.

and if our bodies are neighborhoods,
then, gap junction proteins such as
connexin, coded for by this GJB6 gene,
are like the interwoven streets
connecting the cellular abodes of suburbia.

through these roads and channels,
adjoining biological homes
transport nutrients, forming pathways
to share and shuffle along ions.

it's as if these cellular neighbors
are passing along welcome gift baskets
to newlyweds that just moved in, or
hosting street-wide July 4th barbeques,
or enjoying Super Bowl parties and
Saturday night potlucks filled with
potassium ions and signaling molecules.

wow, cells sure are chummy.
i don't even know half of my neighbors' names.

chromosome 14: 800-900 genes
notable gene: IFT43 gene, intraflagellar transport

wait a minute.
if some cells are stand-alone homes,

then others are RV's and boat houses,
units of life that are transient,
full of wanderlust,
cells topped with finger-like,
moving projections named
cilia and *flagella*
that allow them to explore,
clean the body of impurities,
and activate pathways differently
than stationary junctions.

now, if *we* were our cells,
we'd see that

some of us are nomads -
travelling, exploring the world,
passing IFT particles along
moving cilia,

while others are suburbians -
settling down, and
passing ions in one place,
as gap junctions do.

and many cells use both
in-motion cilia and
stationary junctions.

either way,
they're - we're - all living.

chromosome 15: 600-700 Genes
notable genes: OCA2 & HERC2, eye color

our eyes funnel the chaos of the
world into a tiny, comprehensible picture,

but there is also a world inside them.

if you've ever examined an iris -
i mean, really looked at one up close -
you've seen that a singular color name
is not sufficient to describe the
magnificence of this tiny yet
incredibly important organ.

stories fill the iris. some stories are
told by light-colored eyes that change
from sea foam green to brilliant blue
with shifts in wardrobe and light.

other stories are flecks of hazel and green
and deep brown sparkling with profound
 purpose in the sun's rays, illumination revealing
some majesty that hides beneath a duller
canvas in the absence of brightness.

if you look closely, very closely,
you'll see cosmic stars of colors radiating
from the pupil, displaying all that
those eyes have seen: a snapshot
of someone's life, a fleeting glimpse
into the deepest recesses of the soul
that can't be explained verbally.

zooming in on this vulnerable humanity tells you all you need to
know. it's no surprise that beauty lies in these beholders.

chromosome 16: 800-900 genes
notable gene: MC1R, melanin for hair and skin color

humanity is a rainbow, filled
with a plethora of colors.

sure- it's in our nature to
pick apart. categorize.
assign different names.

in the end, though, the
same two pigments in
varying combinations -
eumelanin and pheomelanin -
are responsible for the coloration
of every person on earth,
whether we're discussing
fiery red hair or
glowing cocoa skin,
deep brown locks or
olive and alabaster visages.

how magical and staggering it is,
that small changes in just
a few little biochemicals
are responsible for so much
historical division,
progressive unity and
universal beauty.

chromosome 17: 1200-1300 genes
notable gene: TP53, tumor suppressor

TP53, biologists call you the guardian of the genome,
but i think you're more of a peacekeeper.

oh tireless public servant,
keeping our cells from dividing
uncontrollably, keeping all
of our anatomical citizens in check.

but...on the days you are off-duty
our biological motors
run haywire. cells roam
with anarchy, accumulating
in the recesses of our systems.

half of all cancers can trace their
source back to mutations in you,
and with shortcomings on your part

unstoppable growth takes over
the domain, with terrifying words like
tumors and *metastasizing* becoming
part of everyday vocabulary.

but guardian. i wish all humans could pay you
more than the measly sum you earn now,
i wish we could give you the credit
you deserve. i wish we could see you
in person now and say *thank you*
for overseeing the working parts of us.

i wish that everyone could recognize
your hard work when things are going right,
and not just quickly admonish you for your faults
when we notice that things are going wrong.

chromosome 18: 200-300 genes
notable gene: CHMP1B, nucleus organization

if DNA can form the template
for proteins that organize
the nucleus-
the veritable brain of
each of our cells, a most
complex part of our
anatomy;

if Henry Ford could create
the moving assembly line
to organize production
all the way back in 1913;

if there exist a plethora of
organization apps,
decorated planners,
and color-coded calendars
in the halls of Target
and the pixelated shelves of
the app store, why do we
fallible humans still
buckle in fear of and
positively fail in the
battle of keeping true

to a
simple,
(un)daunting,
organized to-do list?

chromosome 19: 1500 genes
notable gene: CACNA1C, calcium channels

have you ever wondered exactly
why mother touted the importance
of calcium?

maybe she didn't even
know it, but

other than strong bones and
Got Milk? commercials, humans have
special channels that transport
calcium ions across the cell membrane-
and these channels, found in
every human cell, are vital for
producing electrical signals,
that initiate everything
from muscle contraction
to immune system activation;
they allow our neurons to
speak to one another,
sending neurotransmitters
between nerve cells at
highway-flying speeds.

without calcium, we'd be a partial of a whole,
unable to think, walk, talk or breathe.

and i guess, directly or indirectly,
without her stubborn insistence
and wisdom that transcends
even her own knowledge:
without her tough love, or
twinkle-in-the-eye, omniscient advice,
we'd be the same way without mom.

chromosome 20: 500-600 genes
notable gene: OXT, oxytocin production

oxytocin, that familiar hormone colloquially
cited by scientists and non-scientists alike
as the "love" hormone, the trust hormone,
that substance encapsulating empathy,
well-being, satisfaction,
happiness.

we spend our whole lives looking for that elusive word.

we look for it in salaries, in money,
in job security, in our children.
dreams littered with power and legacies,
tattered songs of relationships and
summer road trips with friends,
endless art about love, being sheltered
amongst the navy freckled skies on a
warm spring night: all of our actions
culminate in this singular quest for the
most subjective, abstract goal imaginable.

perhaps we'll never verbally admit this
underlying thread, but all everyone wants
is to reach happiness.

and no matter how or where we search for it,
the truth is that it's written in our inheritance,
and it's described by our biology, whether it's
in a gene, a hormone, a mind, or a heart...

we must find our happiness inside.

chromosome 21: 200-300 genes
notable gene: APP, precursor for Alzheimer's Disease

be thankful for your well-functioning brain.

find solace in the fact that
you can remember important
anniversaries or birthdays without
a calendar or a reminder.

smile at the idea that
memories are safely tucked in
the corners of your cortex-
sure, you might take pictures
for backup, but right now, flashes
of pixelated recollections are
more secure in your mind
than they'd be in a digital time capsule
that is just waiting to glitch or delete
or run out of storage.

at this very moment in time,
cherish your brain, your ability
to recall your loved ones' names.

at this very moment in time,
there's no use in anxiously awaiting
the onset of a disease that transforms
time's granules into quicksand,
helplessly accelerating every morning,
taking with it remnants of
personality and a full lifetime-

so despite those possibilities, we can't live in fear,
because fear is no way to live.

but we can live in gratitude.

chromosome 22: 500-600 genes
notable gene: SOX10, determinant of cell fate

greek mythology's three most
infamous sisters: Clotho, to
spin the thread; Lachesis, to
draw it, determining its length,
and Atropos, to finally cut the strand.

the Fates controlled the existence
of a mortal, from birth to death,

and SOX10, with a host of
other family members, would be
the biochemical equivalent,
determining cell destiny.

by cutting threads of
proteins and molecules, they
relay which cells specialize
into other types, instructing the
development of the varieties
that stretch from your spinal cord
to every inch of your body;
some even branch off to become
the melanocytes that fill in the
colors of our outlined pages.

but if we have proven that
our biology determines the
destiny of each cell that
composes us, must
we have a
human destiny as well?

or are we greater
than the sum of our parts?

x, y, and

epigenetics

X Chromosome

typically, females have two X chromosomes.

and on this chromosome, surely
we must see the trademark of
progress, notations of how just
decades ago women could not hold
jobs in some of the workplaces
they now manage and run and start up-

but progression does not
equal perfection.

it is not a sign to ignore
the woman caught in the greedy crosshairs
of a coworker's glare, a coworker
seeking to exchange her ambition for
tasteless jokes and subtle discrimination.

it is certainly not a sign to ignore
the women on the other side of
the globe that fight for the right to vote,
work, marry, or divorce without the
permission of a man that sees her as
sub-human, just because of her chromosomes;

or those who still combat the society that
physically quarantines women for days on end
because menstruation is surely "unclean";

or those still fighting to be heard
and to secure the most basic level
of human respect and human rights.

progress
is not localized to the Western world
of ivory towers and pity, and
progress
no matter where it is, is not a finish line.

Y Chromosome

typically, men have one X and one Y chromosome.

and on this Y chromosome, we see the gene
for bravado, coding for a protein that suppresses
emotion just as other genes suppress tumors,

right? well, put that way, it's obviously absurd-

yet somewhere along the way, humans decided
that masculinity was synonymous with *no tears*:
constant ability to weather the world with no weakness.

why do we judge men for simply having feelings?
why do we teach young boys to *man up*,
and reinforce this idea, to the point
where we start believing that men can't
even be abused, physically or emotionally?

is this Y chromosome a magic shield
impervious to all the world's ills? and today,

we excellently encourage girls to pursue
careers in male-dominated fields like STEM,
but did we forget something?

why did we fail to create a "Boys in Humanities" club,
or normalize "Men in Nursing" symposiums?
has our society conditioned males to think that
jobs like these are a blatant affront to masculinity?

why do we say that
women aren't weak- they can be strong!
while men only have the choice of the latter?

why does our world ensure that men everywhere feel
helplessly cordoned into the confines of an abstract ideal?
equality is a two-way street, and too many still drive with blinders.

epigenetics

I.

with *epi* meaning "above",
epigenetics are akin to pencil markings
that float atop the permanent ink
of our inherited DNA.

these fleeting annotations to
our rigid story can be acquired through
environment, behavior, and a cluster
of other factors, and instruct,
through a myriad of methods,
how much or how little the
different parts of our genome
should be expressed- so while
our inheritance cannot actually change
from its code of A, G, T, and C,
these epigenetics edits can
wrap around our DNA and
turn specific traits *on* or *off*.

such graphite modifications can
be erased as crudely as they are
scratched on, but we can also pass on
these faint tracings to future
generations to discover.

this epigenetics is a live scoreboard,
a record-keeper taking your
experiences into account to
edit an unchangeable genome;
and perhaps we here find proof
that DNA, your rigid biological
blueprints, are not your destiny.

rather, we are the ones in control.
most of the time.

II.

if behavioral epigenetics -
the study of how lifestyle affects genetics,
the study of how nurture *affects* nature -
is indeed true, then perhaps
scientists have already discovered
the mechanism for karma. and

by that i mean, if your
epigenome keeps a tally-marked
record of your actions and diet
and circumstances and choices,

perhaps what "goes around" in the
atmosphere surrounding your life
"comes around" to modify the
biochemical stuff that makes you,
and, in turn, the biochemical stuff
that will make up all the generations
that are to succeed you,

and perhaps that is the
greatest karma of all.

III.

a couple of years ago, newspapers
released headlines screaming that
You May Have the Fat Gene,
which supposedly made carriers
helpless slaves of a slow metabolism
and resistant to the benefits
of exercise, effectively rendering
all attempts at a healthy lifestyle
useless. but those headlines,
in their sensational search for
impulse-induced subscriptions,

forgot about epigenetics.

sure, you may have been
unfairly bestowed with a gene
that makes you less likely
to have the slim physique
of your enviable neighbor;
but you, yourself, may be able
to annotate your destiny
of this biological "curse"
through healthy mannerisms.

you are the only one that can
fully control your destiny of
well-being by diminishing
the effects of said "fat gene".

your DNA is not an unchangeable
blueprint- it's merely a sketch
waiting for your hand to fill
in the blanks, so

with healthy actions and
a healthy mindset, pursue the
life that you want to live,

without fears of genetic
inadequacy,

and even if you cannot reach
that ideal by managing your
epigenetics; even if you cannot
ever be that slim neighbor;
even if you fail to live up
to an foggy ideal born in
your mind and perpetrated
by a judging society,

be who you want to be,
regardless of one little

"fat" gene, because we are
all more than our DNA.

IV.

a landmark study of epigenetics
once found that mother mice
who ate a certain diet saw
significant modification epigenetically,
to the point where they passed on genes
that changed the fur color of their
their offspring.

and this study inspired billions
of hopeful epigeneticists,
that they could discover some
parallel events in humans,
and you have to wonder,

if our DNA is more than a
mere mouse's, or if that
even matters. because
we are still wondering
if our humanity is even found
in special double helixes
with certain genes,
or if it lies in the soul
(or lack thereof).

V.

a study that still periodically circulates
its way around headlines reads
*Holocaust Trauma Can
Be Transmitted Epigenetically,*
striking fear into the hearts of
millions of readers who
were just learning about the
implications of this theory,

inciting a world of possibility

on an unstable basis.

look now and you'll see the
claims being debunked.

this study, which, upon its release,
sent the buzzword of *epigenetics*
through the stratosphere, fell
prey to scientific faults:

small sample size. failure to
look at more than one
generational transmission.

the study claimed that this
horrid trauma caused such damage
to a survivor's epigenome that
their children were more likely
to suffer from PTSD or more
susceptible to nightmares,

but how do you separate the
effects of terrible tales
relayed in childhood by
surviving relatives, from the
effects of epigenetics?

was their epigenome really
modified by their parents'
experiences, or did these children
just grow up in a household more
susceptible to and aware of the finer
horrors of human capabilities?

maybe the science will never
be perfect, and maybe
we will never know how much
our experiences biologically

influence our children,
and maybe we'll never know
how much control we have over
our DNA,

but maybe we just live each
day as if we have it tightly
wrapped around our pinky finger,
genome and epigenome both,
with their secrets whispering
only to our unfathoming minds,
so we can synthesize the
feeling of control over the
uncontrollable, no matter
how destined it all may be.

to learn

more . . .

works cited

Olena, A. (2018, March 22). Mouse Moms' Behavior Affects Pups' Genome Structures. *The Scientist.* Retrieved March 30, 2018, from https://www.the-scientist.com/

this article, along with many others also found on The Scientist, *is a fascinating discovery into a facet of epigenetic influence.*

National Library of Medicine (US). Genetics Home Reference [Internet]. Bethesda (MD): The Library; 2018 Mar 27 [cited 2018 Apr 01]. Available from: https://ghr.nlm.nih.gov/.

using mainly this site, i found specific information regarding chromosomes, genetic traits, and more. the database is clearly organized and written in layman's terms – not specific biological jargon - making it easy to explore, for anyone with the slightest curiosity.

Yasmin, S. (2017, June 09). Experts debunk study that found Holocaust trauma is inherited. *Chicago Tribune.* Retrieved March 29, 2018, from http://www.chicagotribune.com/lifestyles/health/ct-holocaust-trauma-not-inherited-20170609-story.html

this article inspired me to create the last piece regarding epigenetics. i always thought the implications regarding this concept were fascinating; but when i found that the study was not totally comprehensive my imagination felt slighted. however, behavioral epigenetics provides an incredible new window through which to gaze at human activity, at nature and nurture. while one study may not concretely set all its mysteries, there is something to be said about the paradigm-shifting possibilities of epigenetics- this one topic alone can inspire so much research, discovery, questioning, and art.

about the author

shruthi n. shivkumar is an aspiring writer and scientist. she finds solace in analyzing her world quantitatively and qualitatively, and seeks to bridge the gap between the sciences and humanities.

this is her first chapbook. her work, including poetry, flash fiction, science fiction, and nonfiction, has been previously recognized by the scholastic art and writing awards at the national level, the johns hopkins creative minds youth magazine, and pta reflections.

she was born in los angeles and raised in the pittsburgh area, and is proudly indian-american. she owes it to her wonderful family and local hindu temple for shaping her positive mindset and giving her the confidence to explore her own identity. she has also written for the pittsburgh patrika - a magazine for indian-americans in the region – and hopes to continue writing for it.

shruthi will be attending the university of pittsburgh starting in the fall of 2018, where she plans to study various topics, ranging from neuroscience to biology to philosophy to writing. in her future, she hopes to unite all the fields above via a diverse career in medicine, public health, and science communication.

she's obsessed with the color that comprises the cover of this book ("turquoise with a hint of sea green", because names are important) and loves crafting, dancing, and singing.

at any given time, you can probably find her creating or daydreaming.